EVERYDAY INSPI

Lexie Bebbington

Copyright © 2017 LEXIE BEBBINGTON. All rights reserved. No portion of this book may be reproduced mechanically, electronically, or by any other means, including photocopying, without written permission of the publisher. It is illegal to copy this book, post it to a website, or distribute it by any other means without permission from the publisher.

    Lexie Bebbington
    Bournemouth
    Email: lexiebebbington@gmail.com

Limits of Liability and Disclaimer of Warranty
The author and publisher shall not be liable for your misuse of this material. This book is strictly for informational and educational purposes.

Warning – Disclaimer
The purpose of this book is to educate and entertain. The author and/or publisher do not guarantee that anyone following these techniques, suggestions, tips, ideas, or strategies will become successful. The author and/or publisher shall have neither liability nor responsibility to anyone with respect to any loss or damage caused, or alleged to be caused, directly or indirectly by the information contained in this book.

To Martin,
With my love and deep appreciation.
You are my rock.

ACKNOWLEDGEMENTS

I would like to say a heartfelt thank you to all the people in my life who have given me so much encouragement and support over the years. With such great people willing me to succeed, I have found the courage to follow my dreams time and time again. And each time, it has become a little easier. I have found an inner strength I never would have discovered, without having been encouraged to push beyond my comfortable, safe boundaries. And yet, just beyond those boundaries, beyond where I believed it was safe for me to go, is where I have often felt the most alive.

I have noticed that this is also true for my clients – and I would like to take this opportunity to thank each and every one of them for inviting me to escort them on their journeys. I have witnessed immense courage and determination, and seen first hand what is possible when we deliberately choose to step confidently in the direction of our dreams. You are my inspiration.

ABOUT THE AUTHOR

With her BSc (Hons) degree in Education, Lexie is a long-time student of the way in which thought, feelings and beliefs structure our lives. She qualified as a Life Coach with Achievement Specialists, who are accredited by the European Coaching Institute, and is also a Certified Professional Co-Active Coach with one of America's leading coaching institutes – C.T.I. Lexie is a published writer and workshop leader, a lover of inspirational quotes and a hair product junkie. She lives in Bournemouth with her husband and their young son.

INTRODUCTION

I have read literally hundreds of self-development books and have attended many courses, completed all kinds of programs and worked my way through plenty of exercises – only to find that my energy dwindles and my motivation fades as soon as other stuff sneaks in and begins to make demands on my time. Let's face it, most of us can find it hard to keep up momentum on our own. We start off full of wonderful ideas and brilliant plans, but then life sort of gets in the way and we can feel like we have let ourselves down by not keeping up with our affirmations and vision boards and journal writing and positive thinking. We want to, we *mean* to… and yet, somehow things start to slip.

With this in mind, I set myself the task of creating a way to encourage us to stay on track easily and effortlessly, no matter how busy life gets. After all, I know how much better we feel when we do! As a coach, I have noticed that finding ways to stay on track when life gets in the way does wonders for our self-esteem and confidence. Unfortunately, old habits die hard – and negative patterns have an irritating habit of sneaking back in whilst our attention is turned … unless we put structures in place to ensure we keep our focus.

So, here it is. A book that requires no more than ten minutes a day of your time, to have real value. Just this one small daily dose could make all the difference to the way you choose to think. This book includes many quotes from inspiring people who have the ability to uplift, to motivate, to inspire – and sometimes, to even overturn our limiting beliefs.

Just selecting a quote each day at random will help to keep you on track. For those of you who want a little more, each quote is followed by an action step, so that you can apply the wisdom to your own life. Enjoy!

"I'm trying to be myself more and more. The more confidence you have in yourself the more you realise that this is you, and life isn't long. So get on with it!"
~ Kylie Minogue

Action Step

Many of us have moments when we doubt ourselves - when that little gremlin in our head tells us that we are not good enough or funny enough or special enough.

Take a moment today to thank your gremlin for showing up – and then tell it firmly but gently that you are now an adult and can make your own decisions. Deliberately do something new or different today, to remind your gremlin who is boss.

"Forgive all who have offended you, not for them, but for yourself."

~ Harriet Nelson

Action Step

Write a letter to a person who has offended you. In the letter, write about your resentment from the perspective of what YOU can be responsible for. What part did you play in creating the situation? How could you have handled it better? What have you learned that will be useful as you move forward in your life?

Clearly state your willingness to forgive the other person, which simply means allowing yourself to let go of the negative emotion. Begin the process of letting go by ripping up the letter or burning it as a ceremonial release.

"It is never too late to be who you might have been."

~ *George Eliot*

Action Step

It is never too late to think about how you might want to enhance the quality of your life. The best place to start is right here. The only time to begin is now. Make a list of the various aspects of your life, such as: Career, Money, Relationships, Friends, Family, Health and Spirituality.

Score each area out of ten, with ten being very satisfied and one being unsatisfied. Now think of one small, manageable action you can take to improve each aspect of your life. Commit to doing each one. Just taking responsibility for completing one small step at a time can lead to powerful, sustainable change – not just in the quality of your life in general, but also in your confidence and your outlook.

"Do or do not. There is no try."
    ~Yoda in 'The Empire Strikes Back'

Action Step

For today, replace the word "try" with a more powerful word, such as "will" or "choose". "I will" or "I choose" lets your subconscious mind know that you are serious about what you are committing to – and that your goals and dreams really matter. If you genuinely don't want to commit to something, you are far more in integrity if you just say a polite "no".

What will you choose to commit to today?

"Goals are dreams with deadlines."
       ~ *Diana Scharf Hunt*

Action Step

Make a list of all your dreams. If you enjoy a challenge, aim for 100. Include all the little, easy dreams along with the big, life changing ones. Include dreams relating to what you would like to experience, as well as things you want to have. Once they are all down, highlight the ones you genuinely want to make real and then set a realistic deadline for each. You have now taken an important step towards transforming your dreams into achievable goals - congratulations!

You may be surprised at the momentum you can create by taking this one simple step.

"Action is the antidote to despair."
 ~ *Joan Baez*

Action Step

When you are feeling disheartened, it doesn't really matter what action you take – as long as you deliberately choose to do something. Taking action helps soothe despair and is a powerful force in rekindling hope. It turns our attention from the problem and redirects it towards possible solutions. The action could be as simple as taking a walk in the park to clear the cobwebs, or it could be as specific as creating a detailed action plan to follow over the next few weeks.

Just commit to doing something… and then do it.

"Turn your face to the sun and the shadows fall behind you."

~ *Maori Proverb*

Action Step

Take a moment to check in with yourself and notice how you are feeling. Just for today, deliberately notice where you put your attention. Do you focus on what is great about your day? Is your glass half full or half empty? Or do you find your mind wandering off into the shadows? Without judgment, allow yourself to become aware of the impact this has on how you feel.

Write about your discoveries in a journal, and use these new insights to help you walk on the brighter side of life.

"If a home doesn't make sense, nothing does."
  ~ *Henrietta Ripperger*

Action Step

How do you feel when you step into your home? Is it a place where you feel safe and secure, happy and relaxed? Is it a space you enjoy spending time? Is your home warm and welcoming?

Take a really good look around your home, and notice whether it reflects who you are. Does it make you feel good to be there? Is your home a place you feel happy to invite friends and loved ones?

Today, make a list of five things you could alter in your home to make it feel better. It might be a case of removing some clutter, buying great cushions for your sofa or adding a splash of colour with some fresh flowers.

*"There came a time when the risk to
remain tight in the bud
was more painful
than the risk it took to blossom."*
~ *Anais Nin*

Action Step

Spend about five minutes focusing your mind on your desires, goals and intentions. Remind yourself that you deserve to live a life of your choosing, even if it feels a little overwhelming to get started. Close your eyes and visualize your goals and desires as already being fulfilled.

Really *feel* the emotions, as if you are already living your dreams. Notice the tension flood out of your body as you allow your dreams to flourish in your imagination. When you feel happy and positive on the inside, you become a magnet for wonderful experiences on the outside, in the real world.

Notice how much more alive you feel when you dare to allow yourself to open up and dream.

"People are not disturbed by things, but by the view they take of them."

~ Epictetus

Action Step

Consciously do something today that opens up a new, fresh perspective or brightens your mood. When we are in a positive mood, everything tends to look a little brighter and more manageable. Some ideas include:

- listening to some music you love,
- going out for a walk in nature
- reading an inspiring book
- phoning an inspiring friend for a chat

Do something today to make yourself feel better – and notice the impact it has on how you view life in general.

*"The difference between
try and triumph
is just a little umph."*
                    ~ Author Unknown

Action Step

If you feel yourself losing momentum before you've reached your goal, it might be time to add a little "umph". Some simple ways to get back on track include:

- Making your goals real by writing them down
- Setting yourself a deadline
- Telling a friend about your goal, so that you can be held accountable
- Breaking your goal down into manageable sized chunks
- Reminding yourself why you set this goal in the first place

Add a little "umph" and soon that sense of triumph will be yours!

"Even if you are on the right track, you'll get run over if you just sit there."

~ *Will Rogers*

Action Step

Sometimes, even when we know we are on the right track, we can suddenly feel immobilized by fear or overwhelmed. We all know that our thoughts literally affect the way we feel. Our biggest fear is of fear itself and the greatest antidote to fear is boldness. Reassure yourself that FEAR is really only a mnemonic for:

False
Evidence
Appearing
Real

What action can you take today to get yourself moving boldly in the direction of your goals?

It is time to take a deep breath – and just do it!

*"Be not afraid of going slowly;
be only afraid of standing still."*
~ *Chinese Proverb*

Action Step

Sometimes it is hard to find the energy and motivation to hit the road running. If you are feeling under the weather, remind yourself that it is more than OK to take your day one small step at a time. Concentrate on the immediate task at hand. When that job is complete, move onto the next one.

Be gentle with yourself, and remember to give yourself acknowledgement for the fact that you are moving in the right direction.

One step at a time is more than good enough.

*"If you think you can, you can.
And if you think you can't,
you're right."*

~ Henry Ford

Action Step

Before attempting anything, it is important to anchor yourself in a state of possibility. If you don't believe you can achieve what you want to achieve, you are most likely to prove yourself right.

Today, take a couple of minutes to remind yourself why you want to achieve your goals – and deliberately step into a mind state where you allow yourself to believe it is possible. Then, choose a task that you know you can do, and do it.

"Fear is a darkroom where negatives develop."

~ *Usman B. Asif*

Action Step

Fear is uncomfortable and can prevent us from moving forward. Once our thoughts begin to focus on things that worry or frighten us, they can spiral out of control and lead to a state of paralysis. A powerful antidote to fear is learning how to choose to "act" instead of "react".

One way to do this is to deliberately choose to focus on something pleasant instead. The next time you experience something that makes you feel good (such as a rainbow, a child giggling or a beautiful sunset), give yourself a moment to commit it to memory. Really allow yourself to absorb the "feel good" feelings.

Then next time you feel "fear" worming its way in, deliberately choose to replay your "feel good" video in your head. This acts as a soothing lotion for the mind.

"Anything I've ever done that was ultimately worthwhile… initially scared me to death."

~ Betty Bender

Action Step

It is perfectly natural to feel worried or nervous about trying something new – but we shouldn't let that stop us. Those gut feelings, dreams and desires you've been experiencing represent the germination of new projects and goals that are calling for your attention.

Just for today, take at least one step in the direction of making your dreams and desires a reality. Even a tiny step that is remotely related to improving your life will make you feel good.

What can you do today to get started?

"I am where I am because I believe in possibilities."

~ Whoopi Goldberg

Action Step

Life is full of ups and downs, but we always have a choice about how we respond to what happens. Just for this week, see everything in your life as an opportunity. Seek new possibilities, no matter what life has to offer. Instead of thinking in terms of "success" and "failure", become a detective and collect all the "data" without judgment.

Set yourself the task of uncovering all the wonderful possibilities that may have eluded you before.

See your life experiences through fresh eyes.

వళవళవళ

"Miracles happen to those who believe in them."

~ *Bernard Berenson*

Action Step

As you go through your day, keep yourself open to the possibility of experiencing amazing or wonderful occurrences. Wholeheartedly believe that wonderful things are in store for you. The more you allow yourself to believe in miracles, the more you will experience them in your day to day life.

Take a moment to fine tune your senses to take in the awesome miracles that occur every day, but are often passed unnoticed: a glorious pink sunrise, the hug of a loved one, the wonder of sight, the sound of great music or the smell of freshly cut grass.

༄༄༄

*"The two best physicians
of them all -
Dr Laughter and Dr Sleep."*
~ Gregory Dean

Action Step

Laughter really is the best medicine. Today, deliberately choose to do something that makes you belly laugh. Perhaps it is watching a funny movie or spending time with great friends. Whatever it is, let yourself laugh until your sides ache.

To ensure that you squeeze the most value out of your belly laugh medicine, follow it with an early night or two.

A couple of nights where you are in bed by 9pm can work wonders!

༄༄༄

"The best thing about the future is that it only comes one day at a time."

~ Abraham Lincoln

Action Step

Once you have some clarity about your long term and medium term goals, take a moment to stop and smell the roses. The present moment is all we ever really have. We cannot live in the past or the future. The only moment we ever get to live in is this one.

Whenever you feel that you are worrying about the future or concerned with some aspect of the past, take a deep breath and pause for a moment. Allow your awareness to drop down into your body and experience a deeper sense of who you are.

Appreciate this precious moment of your life.

"Expecting the world to treat
you fairly because you are
a good person
is a little like expecting
the bull not to attack you because
you are a vegetarian."
~ Dennis Wholey

Action Step

It is not the job of the world to treat us fairly, it is *our* job to treat *ourselves* with kindness. When we treat ourselves with love and respect, the world reflects this back. The world is our mirror, and will always give us what we believe we deserve and expect to receive.

Do you treat yourself in a caring way? Could you be more loving and encouraging with yourself? Just for today, make a conscious effort to treat yourself with the same level of love, care and respect that you give to the people in your life that you love.

Nurture yourself and notice how the world will begin to nurture you more too.

৵৵৵

*"The weak can never forgive.
Forgiveness is the
attitude of the strong."*
~ *Mahatma Gandhi*

Action Step

Forgiveness is far from easy. It ironically feels more natural to hold onto the anger and resentment, and we believe it will keep us safe from being hurt further. The truth, however, is the exact opposite.

Those feelings of anger and resentment can fester within us, and actually make us ill. Forgiving someone is an act you do for yourself. It releases you from those festering emotions and sets you free. Forgiving someone takes strength and courage – but it *is* possible, and feels incredibly liberating.

Think of someone you feel some resentment towards and take a step towards forgiving them. Use your strength to set yourself free.

"When the Japanese mend broken objects, they aggrandize the damage by filling the cracks with gold. They believe that when something's suffered damage and has a history, it becomes more beautiful."
~ Barbara Bloom

Action Step

We all experience bumps and scrapes (both metaphorical and physical) through this journey we call life.

This quote reminds us that these "cracks" are an integral part of what make us unique. We have had to show courage and strength to dust ourselves down and get up again and again. It is time to acknowledge the strength we have shown – and be proud of ourselves for our determination to keep going, no matter what.

Just for today, treat yourself with deep respect and admiration for all you have been through.

∾∾∾

"It takes one person to change your life – you."

~Ruth Casey

Action Step

You are the person you've been waiting for. Isn't that a relief? There is no-one outside yourself that you need to rely upon to make any changes you want to make. You are your own hero.

Think about three people (real or fictional) that you admire. Make a list of the qualities they have that you rate most highly. The great news is that these qualities also live in you. For you to recognize these traits, you must also have them within you.

Just for today, select a couple of the qualities that appeal to you most and deliberately choose ways to live them more fully.

*"Faith is taking the first step,
even when you don't see
the whole staircase."*
     ~ *Martin Luther King Jr.*

Action Step

One step is all you need to take you in the direction of your dreams, goals and desires. One act of courage, one shift in perception, one decision, one opportunity. The world mirrors your intention, your trust and your faith. Either you wait, or you decide to take that first step.

Today, ask yourself, "What is that first step?" Listen to your intuition and get started. Don't worry about how you will reach the top of the staircase – the way will reveal itself to you step by step. All you need to do is begin.

Have faith in yourself and the process - and begin it now.

৶৶৶

"Change your thoughts and you change your world."
~ *Norman Vincent Peale*

Action Step

Thoughts are powerful things – you attract whatever you give your attention to, whether positive or negative. Just for today, remind yourself how empowering it can be to think positive thoughts and to deliberately focus on feeling good. What three things can you add to your day to make yourself feel joyful?

You might even want to keep a list of things you enjoy doing, so that you can refer to it whenever you need a bit of a boost and want to brighten your day, your life… and your world.

ঔঔঔ

"If you don't know where you are going, you will probably end up somewhere else."

~ Lawrence J. Peter

Action Step

Spend a few minutes visualizing the most fulfilled vision of your life. What will you be doing? Who will you be with? What lights you up in this vision of yourself? How will you be spending your days? What are you wearing? How are you *being*? The more clarity you can have around your future, the more likely it is that you will head in the direction of your dreams.

After all, how can you head towards something you want, until you are clear about what that is?

☙☙☙

"Every survival kit should include a sense of humour."
            ~ Author Unknown

Action Step

A sense of humour helps you play with different perceptions, entertain quirky ideas, shift your thinking and open your mind to new opportunities. Next time you feel that you are entering a difficult situation, check that you have included a sense of humour in your survival kit. Always be open to finding the funny side of any given situation.

Humour is a state of mind. The trick is to deliberately choose it, rather than let fear, worry or anger find you instead. Humour is a gateway to laughter – and laughter opens the doorway to feeling good, no matter what.

Just for today, be open to finding the humour in everyday situations and circumstances. Notice how it feels to know this is a choice that is always available to you in any given moment.

༄༄༄

"An affirmation is a strong, positive statement that something is already so."
      ~ Shakti Gawain

Action Step

We can choose to use positive affirmations to nourish ourselves emotionally and make us feel good about ourselves and our lives. Affirmations are always stated in the present tense using the first person pronoun, "I". For example:

- I like myself and I am proud to be me.
- I am loving, loveable and loved.
- I am safe, happy and secure.
- Every day, I am becoming more confident and self-assured.

Today, create three affirmations for yourself. Be sure to only use positive words or phrases which describe what you truly want to experience. Write them on a piece of card and carry them with you. Repeat them regularly to yourself, as the repetition is important for the words to really sink in to your subconscious mind.

Affirmations are a powerful addition to your confidence building tool kit. Use daily for best results.

*"Gratitude helps you to
grow and expand;
gratitude brings joy and laughter
into your life and the lives
of those around you."*
                              ~ Eileen Caddy

Action Step

If there is one thing that can make a significant difference to how you feel on a daily basis, it is deliberately choosing to notice things in your life you can feel grateful for, no matter how challenging or difficult that might seem. Of course, it is easier to feel gratitude when things are going really well – but finding something to feel grateful for is an option that is always available to us. The reward is feeling good, no matter what.

Today, find yourself a small pebble or stone and carry it in your pocket. Every time you touch it, use it as a tangible reminder to stop and think about something you can feel grateful for.

Take a moment to really let yourself *feel* the positive emotion.

*"We don't stop playing because
we grow old;
We grow old because
we stop playing."*
~ *George Bernard Shaw*

Action Step

When was the last time you found time for play? When life gets busy and responsibilities pile up, play is something that often tends to slip off the radar. Today, make a list of ten things that you find fun. Do you enjoy playing golf? Tennis? Feeding bread to ducks? Going for an invigorating walk first thing in the morning? Playing rounders on the beach with a group of friends? Kicking through dry, crunchy, Autumn leaves?

Commit to finding the time to add some lighthearted fun to your life, at least twice a week.

Fun people can be any age – staying young is an attitude and has nothing to do with how old we are.

෴෴෴

"The thing tends to happen that you really believe in; and the belief in a thing makes it happen."
~ Frank Lloyd Wright

Action Step

Our minds are like magnets which always attract what they choose to focus on and believe in. Unfortunately, our mental magnets are greatly influenced by our worries and fears, which act as a barrier, preventing the good stuff that we want from getting through.

If you are focusing on what you want in life, you will most likely be excited and energized. When you focus on your worries and fears, you may notice that you feel drained and defeated.

With this in mind, just for today, deliberately and consciously turn your attention to what you want. Feel the anticipation and excitement begin to build. These sensations are a powerful indication that you are charging your mind with mental energy and building up your power of attraction.

❦❦❦

"The distance is nothing;
it is only the first step
that is difficult."
~ Marie de Vichy-Chamrond

Action Step

I have noticed that whenever I decide to go out for a run, the hardest part of the entire process seems to be putting my trainers on! The internal battle I have with myself to get out the house is quite a struggle. Then once I am outdoors, the actual jogging is really quite enjoyable.

Beginning something is often the hardest part. The initial push to get started always requires more energy than keeping it going. Once in motion, much less effort is required to keep up the momentum. With this in mind, what one small thing can you do today to get the ball rolling?

What is your equivalent of putting on your trainers?

❧❧❧

*"For true happiness,
look within yourself.
It is difficult to be happy if you
rely on outside resources."*
~ Keith D. Harrell

Action Step

Before making your "to do" list, make your "to be" list. Spend a few moments getting clear about how you want to show up today. Do you want to be kind, loving, patient, easy going and light hearted? Do you want to be organized and structured in your thinking?

Writing a "to be" list before you begin your "to do" list encourages you to look within for your emotional stability. It reminds you that you can choose how you want to feel, without needing to rely on resources outside of yourself.

Over time, this process offers you an internal compass, directing how you feel, and consequently influencing what you attract into your life.

༺༺༺

"People take different roads seeking fulfilment and happiness. Just because they're not on your road doesn't mean they've gotten lost."
~ H. Jackson Browne

Action Step

Many of us exhaust ourselves by trying to convince other people to live their lives "our way". We think we know what is best for them, and plough our energy into convincing them that we are right. Just for today, consider the possibility that everyone has their own life path – and that each one is just perfect for the person who is on it. Let go of wanting to "fix" other people, and focus on living your very best life instead.

What one thing can you do today that will make *you* feel happy and fulfilled?

❧❧❧

"This is my 'depressed stance'.
When you're depressed, it makes a lot
of difference how you stand.
The worst thing you can do is
straighten up and hold your head high
because then you'll start to feel better.
If you're going to get any joy
out of being depressed, you've got
to stand like this."

~ Charlie Brown

Action Step

If you are feeling a little low and need a boost, a great place to start is to alter your stance. Take a few moments to stand really straight. Spread your arms out as wide as you can and wiggle your fingertips. Hold your head high and make yourself as tall as you possibly can. Stand on tip toes. Breathe deeply. Smile. Notice how when you change the way you hold yourself physically, your emotions shift too. Add a few star jumps or some fun, energetic dancing for the ultimate pick me up.

Your body finds it hard to remain depressed when it is encouraged to move around.

ৰ্ঞ্চৰ্ঞ্চৰ্ঞ্চ

*"I don't believe people are looking
for the meaning of life
as much as they are looking
for the experience of being alive."*
~ Joseph Campbell

Action Step

Getting clear about what makes you feel fully alive and happy is a surprisingly powerful exercise. Today, spend a few minutes listening to some great music, before settling down to make a list of at least ten things you absolutely love to do. Don't worry if it takes you more than one sitting to complete your list, as this is not a line of enquiry that often gets our full consideration. Take as long as you need to write your ideas down – and let yourself enjoy this process of discovery. Once you are happy with your list, use it as a simple reminder of ways to add more fun and joy to your daily life.

Even as little as five minutes a day of time devoted to yourself can deepen your sense of contentment and make you feel more alive.

༄༄༄

"Sometimes great gifts are not well wrapped. Don't let the wrapping put you off!"

~ *Robert Holden*

Action Step

Practise seeing everything in your life as an opportunity – a gift designed to support you through the process of achieving your dreams and goals. Even when the wrapping looks a little ominous, ask yourself, "What is the gift in this situation? How can even *this* be useful?" Things are not always what they seem.

Choose a situation from your life that didn't go quite as planned, and spend a few moments looking for the gift in it. What did you learn about yourself? In what ways did you become stronger or more determined as a result?

How will you choose to use this information in the future?

৯৯৯

*"I am nobody.
Nobody is perfect.
Therefore I am perfect."*
~ Author Unknown

Action Step

There is nothing like a change in perspective when you are feeling a little low, to brighten your day. Change is like a breath of fresh air and can improve your confidence. Just looking at yourself and your world from a different point of view has the ability to provide a significant shift. Allow yourself to consider the possibility that you are perfect. You are perfectly *you*. In fact, no-one else on this planet can be you the way that *you* can.

You have a unique perspective on life that never existed before you were born, and will never be repeated again in all history. Your job is not to compare yourself with anyone else, but to learn how to be deliciously, splendidly YOU.

Choose to do something a little out of the ordinary today in celebration of your quirky, delightfully human self. Make it fun!

֍֍֍

"I was always looking outside myself for strength and confidence but it comes from within. It is there all the time."

~ Anna Freud

Action Step

Confidence is always an inside job, and it is our responsibility to nurture that inner confidence so that it can flourish. We are all born with a healthy regard for ourselves, but unfortunately it often gets challenged as we grow up.

As adults, we just need to find ways to remind ourselves of how special and unique we are. Today, make a list of things that are *right* about you. This list can include anything at all that you feel good about: your strengths, your kindness, your creativity, your sense of humour, your ability to connect with others.

Keep this wonderfully unique list close to hand, and refer to it in moments of self-doubt.

☙☙☙

"I don't think of all the misery but of the beauty that still remains."

~ *Anne Frank*

Action Step

Anne Frank had an amazing capacity to look for beauty in a tormented world. One of the ways she was able to keep her focus was through regular writing in her diary. Journal writing is a very helpful way of directing our attention, rather than letting our thoughts run wild.

Today, I invite you to start keeping a daily gratitude journal. This is not the kind of diary where you write down all the things that have happened. Instead, it is a special place to list five things that you are grateful for on a particular day. There is no right or wrong way to do this – the aim is to support you in keeping your focus and enjoying the feeling of gratitude as you write.

Your list could include such things as a kind word, a gift from a friend, the first signs of Spring, a delicious mug of hot chocolate or being wrapped up warm on a cold, brisk walk.

"There is nothing more genuine than breaking away from the chorus to learn the sound of your own voice."

~ Po Bronson

Action Step

When you spend quality time on your own, you can learn to become still enough to listen to the quiet whisper of your own inner voice. Over time, you will learn the skill of tuning into your intuition, which can be very helpful when it comes to decision making. Most of us deliberately avoid full mental solitude, away from the phone, the TV and books and magazines. It can be uncomfortable to spend time without any mental stimulation, but the benefits can be surprising.

Begin to deliberately carve out small chunks of quality time by yourself – even ten minutes a couple of times a week would make a difference.

Use this time as an opportunity to be curious about yourself – and to sit quietly for a while with only your own thoughts for company.

ఇఇఇ

"Everyone has a 'risk muscle'.
You keep it in shape
by trying new things.
If you don't, it atrophies.
Make a point of using it
at least once a day."
~ Roger Von Oech

Action Step

Many of us keep ourselves safe and warm, tucked up in our homes with a range of electronic gadgets for company. Of course, there are times when "battening down the hatches" and snuggling down with a hot chocolate and some good TV can be a wonderful way to unwind. Too often however, we can become a little over-comfortable in our cocoon, so that risks, adventure and excitement stay firmly off the agenda. When we do this for an extended period, our "risk muscle" atrophies – and we tend to stop "living" and begin to settle for simply "existing" instead.

Today, think about some fun things you might like to try. It could be as simple as going out to eat at a new restaurant, or as exhilarating as learning to skydive. The important thing is to explore new ideas that genuinely appeal to you.

*"Slow down and enjoy life.
It's not only the scenery you miss
by going too fast -
you also miss the sense of
where you are going and why."*
~ Eddie Cantor

Action Step

Remembering to enjoy the journey is at least as important as arriving at the destination. The reality is that a great deal of our life is spent on the journey itself, so it makes sense to enjoy this essential part of the process.

What small tweaks can you make to your life to increase the amount of time you have to just stop and breathe and check in with yourself? Could you consider reducing the number of times you check your email? How about waking up ten minutes earlier? By slowing down a little, we tend to spend more time in the present moment – which can actually also improve our memory. This can then help us save even more time by making us more aware of the little details in life that we often feel the need to double check – such as whether we locked the front door, or where we put the keys.

Just by slowing down a little, you may find life gets a bit easier and more enjoyable.

"Walking is good for solving problems – it's like the feet are little psychiatrists."

~ *Pepper Giardino*

Action Step

Walking more is a great route to improved health and happiness. The mental benefits are just as important as the more obvious physical ones. Walking helps you relax. It releases stress and soothes the mind. It can also offer the quiet we require to connect with our intuition – which in turn can lead us to finding the solutions for problems or discovering fascinating new insights. Today, do whatever it takes to find some time to go for a brisk walk.

Even as little as fifteen minutes will provide you with an energy boost, sharpen your mind, clear the cobwebs and lift your spirits.

৵৵৵

"Kindness in words creates confidence. Kindness in thinking creates profoundness. Kindness in giving creates love."

~ Lao Tzu

Action Step

Being kind to yourself is one of the greatest gifts you not only give to yourself, but also to everyone you come into contact with. When you are kind to yourself, you reflect this back and are kinder to everyone else as well. Today, treat yourself the way you would treat a child you love. With that child you would be patient and kind. You would be fair, whilst setting reasonable boundaries. You can do the same thing for yourself, which will enable you to get through tough times without being self-critical and negative.

Today, find three very definite ways that you can be kind to yourself. It might be reading something inspiring, or treating yourself to a pedicure. Perhaps you could take yourself out for a lovely walk or watch a funny movie. The important thing is to choose three things and ensure you carry them through.

◈◈◈

> "We have two ears
> and only one tongue
> in order that we may
> hear more and speak less."
> ~Diogenes Laertius

Action Step

Most of us are quite uncomfortable with silence, and will talk more than we intend to, simply to avoid silence seeping into our conversations. Sometimes we even finish off each other's sentences and do our best to pre-empt what is going to be said next. And yet, the most powerful way to share a genuine conversation with someone is to really listen.

Give another person space to express themselves, and you may have an opportunity to find out what they really think. Becoming a mindful listener and focusing on what is being said makes conversations flow better – and also makes the other person feel really good. Today, spend a minimum of five minutes in a conversation with someone else where you don't interrupt. Respond with encouraging nods, smiles and looks of understanding. Limit your verbal responses to short phrases such as "I see".

Watch the other person's face light up in appreciation - we all love to feel heard.

"A healthy attitude is contagious, but don't wait to catch it from others. Be a carrier."

~ *Author Unknown*

Action Step

When we are feeling a little low, spending time with genuinely happy and caring people can lift our spirits and help us feel better. But how about when we are on our own and find our mind is beginning a downward spiral? What then?

A simple exercise that can do wonders is to create a list of things that went well during the day. Deliberately choose to focus your attention on all the little things that you found interesting, stimulating, amusing or generally went well. It doesn't matter how small or insignificant these things seem to you – be a detective and search them out. Then let the negative aspects of your day quietly slip off your radar. This exercise encourages you to alter the way you think and feel.

When you focus your attention on things you feel good about, you learn to become a more positive person in your own right.

"If you want to make an easy job seem mighty hard, just keep putting off doing it."
~ *Olin Miller*

Action Step

Thinking about getting started on doing something is almost always a lot harder than actually doing it. We worry about failing or not being able to get started or making a mistake. Our mind spins off into a vortex of fear and failure. Susan Kennedy (aka SARK) has developed a fabulously simple method for overcoming procrastination, called "micromovements".

A "micromovement" is anything from 5 seconds to 5 minutes in length – because we can do just about anything for 5 seconds to 5 minutes. You may find that once you have completed your achievable "micromovement", you suddenly feel energized to continue with your task, which is great! Or, you may find that you need to have a rest and recover. Either way is fine.

The great news is you just did the hardest part and got started – now all you need to do is gently reschedule your next "micromovement".

൞൞൞

*"Consider the postage stamp:
its usefulness consists in the ability
to stick to one thing 'til it
gets there."*

~ Josh Billings

Action Step

Sometimes it can be difficult to stay focused on what we really want to get done, with so many outside influences demanding our attention. We wait for a free moment to get going and yet those moments feel few and far between.

Today, take charge of your schedule. Make a list of your top five priorities, and then write down what needs to be done in ink. It can be helpful to block out chunks of time for yourself in your diary, so that you can honestly say you are busy if other demands are made of you.

It is not so important *what* you specifically do during these times – what is most important is that you *stick* to your plan and feel the immense sense of satisfaction you get from reaching the targets and goals that you set for yourself.

༺༺༺

"Why wait for the weekend to have fun?"

~ *Loesje*

Action Step

There is nearly always something to celebrate if we look hard enough, so why wait until the weekend? Sometimes we procrastinate when it comes to taking the time to have fun, believing that it will cost too much time and money - and yet the benefits may well outweigh the costs. Each of us thrives on fun, connection and laughter.

Although you may wish that someone else would take the initiative to suggest a fun night out, find the time today to plan an enjoyable evening out with your friends or a loved one. It could be as simple as a games evening with a few friends or as romantic as a candle-lit dinner for two.

What can you decide to celebrate today?

※※※

"If someone in your life talked to you the way you talk to yourself, you would have left them long ago."
    ~ *Carla Gordon*

Action Step

Deep down, most of us are very self-critical. Even people who seem to have plenty of confidence have moments of self-doubt, when that irritating little voice in their heads begins a tirade of negative chatter. The next time you hear the voice inside your head, take a moment to give it a comical identity that makes you smile. Use humour as a way of separating the inner critic from yourself.

What will your inner critic look like?

Think of some creative ways to keep it busy when you have had enough of the negative talk. Give it a job to do or send it on an exotic holiday.

Most importantly, learn to value and love yourself instead.

AFTERWORD

I hope you have noticed how an investment of just a couple of minutes a day can make a surprising difference to how you feel. Whenever you open this book and select a quote at random, you are actually giving your subconscious mind something wonderfully tangible to focus on.

You see, for most of us, the subconscious is often switched to default mode, which means that it tends to drift to wherever our everyday worries, niggles and stresses decide to take it. The subconscious then does its job exceptionally well – and unfortunately that job is primarily to look for evidence in our lives to back up our loudest thoughts.

Have you ever had thoughts like these?

- "I always get a cold."
- "I never win at anything!"
- "If I hope for the best, I might jinx it!"
- "If I don't try, I won't be disappointed."
- "I'm too old to start now."
- "I'll never get that promotion."

When we let our conscious minds dwell on worries, problems and negative outcomes, our subconscious assumes we are asking for more of the same and will work hard to ensure that it delivers – even though that is usually the last thing we really want to happen!

But now you have a simple, very practical tool that can change all that. You now know how to reign in your subconscious mind and put yourself back in the driver's seat. Instead of leaving it to chance, you can deliberately choose what your conscious mind thinks about and focuses upon.

The subconscious mind can do amazing work on your behalf when you know how to use it properly – and that is precisely what you are doing when you choose to give it something inspiring to chew on. Suddenly you have given your mind a powerful, positive role to play in making your day a whole lot better.

❖❖❖

NOTES

NOTES